P9-BYO-323

AIRPLANES

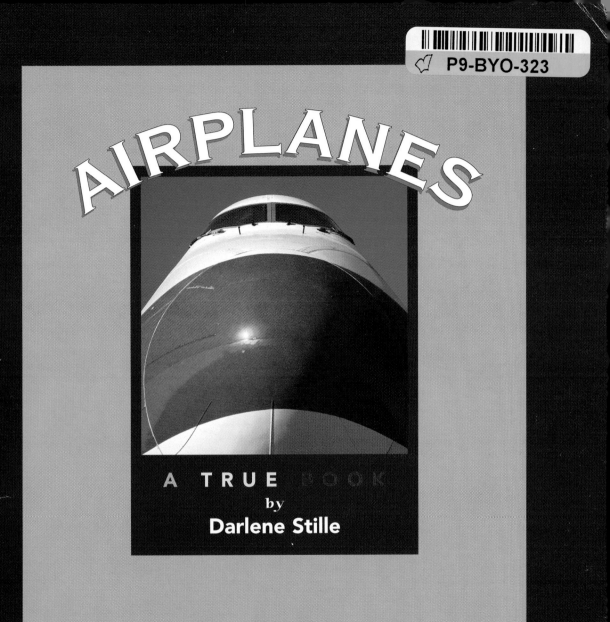

A TRUE BOOK

by

Darlene Stille

Children's Press®
A Division of Grolier Publishing

New York London Hong Kong Sydney
Danbury, Connecticut

Reading Consultant
Linda Cornwell
Learning Resource Consultant
Indiana Department of
Education

Interior of a 777
passenger jet

Library of Congress Cataloging-in-Publication Data

Stille, Darlene
    Airplanes / by Darlene Stille
        p.   cm. — (A true book)
    Includes index.
    Summary: Discusses how planes fly, their parts, and their different
uses.
    ISBN 0-516-20325-8 (lib. binding)   0-516-26161-4 (pbk.)
    1. Airplanes—Juvenile literature. [1. Airplanes.] I. Title. II. Series.
TL547.S83 1997
629.133'34—DC20   96-27211
                                                                              CIP
                                                                              AC

© 1997 Children's Press®, a Division of Grolier Publishing Co., Inc.
All rights reserved. Published simultaneously in Canada.
Printed in the United States of America.
1 2 3 4 5 6 7 8 9 10 R 05 04 03 02 01 00 99 98 97

Contents

Whether they are small or large, all airplanes need wings.

Airplanes

Have you ever gone to the airport and looked at the airplanes? Some are small, some are short, and others are enormous!

Airplanes look different from each other, but they are similar in many ways. For instance, all planes need wings. The wings are attached to the airplane body, also called the fuselage. The very front of the fuselage is the nose. In back of the nose is the cockpit, where the pilot and crew sit. Sticking up at the rear of the fuselage is the tail.

Almost every airplane has wings, a cockpit, a fuselage, and a tail. But each airplane appears different because each airplane has a different job.

Types of Airplanes

Passenger planes carry people, and cargo planes carry freight. Military planes transport soldiers and supplies and fly combat missions.

Airplanes also have different types of engines. Some airplanes have propeller engines that use a propeller to pull the airplane through the air. Others have jet engines. And some have engines called turboprops that use the power of a jet engine to turn a propeller.

Airplanes come in all sizes. The smallest planes are called ultralights. They have one propeller engine and can

Small planes usually fly with propeller engines.

A jumbo jet's engines are attached to its wings (left). A jumbo jet engine under construction (right).

carry one or two people over very short distances. The biggest planes are called jumbo jets. They have three or four jet engines and can carry several hundred people for thousands of miles.

How Airplanes Fly

There are two basic types of aircraft—those that are lighter than air, and those that are heavier than air. Balloons and blimps are lighter-than-air craft that can fly because they are filled with a gas that is lighter than air. But airplanes are made of materials such as

The airplane's engines (left) and wings (right) allow it to fly.

metal and wood. These heavy materials make the airplane heavier than air.

Airplanes can fly because they have engines and wings. The engines make the airplane go fast. When the plane is going fast enough, air rushing over and under the wings creates a force that lifts the plane into the air.

But airplanes need more than wings and engines in order to fly. They need parts to make them turn left, right, up, and down.

One of the most important parts for turning an airplane is the rudder. The rudder is a movable part on the airplane's

This plane's flaps (under the wings) are down as it approaches the runway.

tail, a fin that sticks up from the back of the plane. Other parts that help a plane turn are called ailerons, which are on the edge of the wings.

Parts important for making the plane take off and land are also on the edge of the wings. These parts are called flaps.

Taking Off and Landing

Airplanes need to take off and land on a runway. Most runways are made of concrete, but sometimes planes even land on grassy or open fields.

Before an airplane can take off, it must wait in line with other airplanes for its turn.

A view of a runway from the air

Finally, when the plane is ready to take off, the pilot turns the engines up to full power. The airplane races down the runway. When the airplane is going fast enough, the air rushes under the wings and pushes

The plane begins the take-off by starting down the runway.

the plane up into the sky. Some planes need to travel over 200 miles (321 kilometers) per hour before taking off.

To land, the airplane slowly approaches the runway. The pilot gently lowers the airplane until the wheels touch the runway. But the airplane is still moving very fast. The pilot brakes the wheels and lowers the flaps on the wings. This brings the airplane to a stop.

This jumbo jet needs fourteen wheels to land!

Air Traffic Controllers

Every day, thousands of planes fly overhead. Who keeps track of them all and makes sure everyone is safe?

Air traffic controllers work in offices on the ground and monitor aircraft flights. Closely watching their radar, air traffic controllers tell pilots where it is safe to fly, when it is safe to turn, and when they can fly higher or lower.

Air traffic controllers perform an important job. They keep the skies safe for everyone who flies in a plane.

At the Airport

When passengers arrive at the airport, they take their suitcases to the check-in counter. Suitcases are also called baggage. The passengers check their baggage and get a boarding pass, a piece of paper with a number that tells them where to sit on the plane.

Flight Information

An agent helps a family check in their luggage (above). These passengers are passing though a metal detector (left).

Next, the passengers go to the gate, the place where they board the airplane. Before arriving at the gate, all passengers must walk through a metal detector. The metal detector will alert officials if someone is trying to bring a gun or a bomb onto the plane.

There might be hundreds of passengers waiting to board a jumbo jet. For a small plane, there may only be 15 or 20 passengers. But most planes carry between 100 and 200 passengers.

Passenger and Cargo Planes

Of all the types of planes, the ones we see most often are passenger planes. Passenger planes are owned by airline companies. Some passengers ride planes to vacation spots, and others use them for business trips.

During a flight on a passenger plane, passengers sit in

Passengers board a jet (top). An attendant serves drinks during a flight (bottom).

seats in the body of the plane, called the cabin. Attendants serve snacks and drinks from a tiny kitchen called the galley. On long flights, meals are

Cross section of a passenger jet

served on trays. On very long flights, passengers can even watch a movie.

Cargo planes do not have a passenger cabin with seats. They usually do not have windows in the fuselage.

Instead, there is a big space for boxes and bags and other cargo. Cargo planes have big doors and special machinery for loading cargo.

Airplanes are the fastest way to ship cargo, but they are also the most expensive. Cargo

Important cargo is loaded onto an airplane.

Cross section of a cargo plane (above) and the interior where the cargo is stored (left)

that must be delivered quickly goes on airplanes. Fresh flowers and fresh foods are delivered by air. Packages and mail are often sent on cargo planes, and express mail companies own their own planes.

Most air cargo does not weigh very much. But huge transport planes can carry heavy cargo. These planes can carry big machines. For example, military forces have huge cargo planes to carry trucks and tanks.

Cargo planes can carry heavy military equipment.

Special Planes

Not all planes carry passengers or cargo. There are also planes with special uses. Crop dusters are small propeller planes used to spray bug killers and fertilizers on farm fields. Firefighters ride in special planes designed to fight forest fires. Seaplanes

A plane douses a forest fire with special chemicals (above). Seaplanes use lakes as their runways (left).

are aircraft with large skis that allow them to land on water. Seaplanes carry mail and supplies to people in the Arctic and remote places.

World War II B-17
bomber (below)
B-2 stealth
bomber (right)

Military planes are made for combat. Fighter planes attack enemy aircraft, and bombers drop bombs. Spy planes have cameras for taking pictures of enemy territory. Transport planes carry soldiers and supplies to combat areas, and tankers bring fuel to other planes in the air.

Many planes are owned by airlines or by governments. But there are also private planes that people own for their personal use. The small-est private planes have engines with one propeller. People ride in these planes for short trips or for fun.

People Who Work With Airplanes

Many people work on planes and in airports. The pilot, co-pilot, and sometimes a flight engineer sit in the cockpit and operate the plane's controls. Cabin attendants look out for everyone's safety.

Airline employees who work at the airport are called

A flight crew in a cockpit (top) prepares for takeoff. On the runway, a ground crew member directs the pilot (left).

the ground crew. Some ground crew members use hand signals to guide planes arriving at the airport terminal building. They tell the pilot where to park the plane.

Mechanics work on airplanes in huge hangars (above). A ground crew worker checks an airplane tire (right).

Mechanics check the airplanes. Sometimes they bring the planes into huge buildings called hangars. The mechanics fix any broken parts on the airplanes. Other ground crew members load mail or cargo on and off planes.

The First Airplanes

Long ago, people wanted to fly like the birds. They tried to build machines that would fly.

Two American brothers, Orville and Wilbur Wright, built and flew the first heavier-than-air machine. Their flying machine was made of wood and cloth, and they called it

The Wright brothers (above) flew the first airplane. Daredevil stunts thrilled crowds (left).

The Flyer. The Wright brothers' plane did not fly very far. Its first flight on December 17, 1903, lasted only a few seconds.

But soon other inventors made better planes that could

fly farther and faster. These early airplanes, called biplanes, had two wings, one above the other, and the cockpits were open and exposed to the air.

At first, these planes were used for fun. Pilots raced their planes and tried to see how far they could fly. They performed in shows for people on the ground and did such dangerous stunts as walking on the wings while the plane was in the air.

During World War I (1914–1918), planes had machine guns in front of the cockpit. Military pilots flew the planes on combat missions during World War I. The pilots tried to shoot each other down in dog-fights. Air combat was very dangrous, and many pilots were killed.

After the war, pilots began taking passengers on trips. Bigger airplanes with better engines and enclosed bodies could carry more passengers. They could fly across the ocean. They could fly around the world.

Jet engines, which were first widely used in the late 1950s, made airplanes very popular. Jets could go much faster than propeller-driven planes. Some could go faster than the speed of sound.

Now, millions of people travel on airplanes every year.

Two Great

The early airplanes and the aviators who flew them caught the imagination of the American people in the 1920s and 1930s.

Charles Lindbergh designed a plane to fly across the Atlantic Ocean, and named it the *Spirit of St Louis*. In 1927, he flew from New York City to Paris in about 33 1/2 hours, and became the first person to fly alone across the Atlantic Ocean.

Aviators

In 1932, Amelia Earhart became the first woman to fly across the Atlantic alone. In 1937, Earhart attempted to fly around the world. But while she was flying over the Pacific Ocean, she and her airplane disappeared. Neither she nor her airplane were ever found. But the legend of Amelia Earhart lives on as one of the great pioneers of aviation.

Airplanes of Tomorrow

Inventors are still working on better planes. They want to build planes that go faster. They want a plane that will travel thousands of miles in just one hour.

This plane, called a hypersonic plane, would move five times faster than sound. To do this, it would go up very high. And while the plane was traveling

With the help of modern computers, inventors may soon build a plane that can travel to the edge of space.

toward its destination through Earth's atmosphere, the Earth would be turning below it, bringing the destination closer to the plane. A hypersonic plane might fly from New York City to Tokyo in three or four hours.

This new type of plane would carry its passengers right to the edge of space.

To Find Out More

Here are some additional sources to help you learn more about airplanes:

 **Books**

 **Organizations**

Baxter, Leon. **Famous Flying Machines.** Hambleton-Hill, 1992.

Evans, Frank. **All Aboard Airplanes.** Putnam, 1994.

Gunning, Thomas. **Dream Planes.** Macmillan, 1992.

Pearl, Lizzy. **The Story of Flight.** Troll, 1993.

Richardson, Joy. **Airplanes.** Watts, 1994.

Academy of Model Aeronautics
5151 East Memorial Drive
Muncie, Indiana 47302

American Aviation Historical Society
2333 Otis Street
Santa Ana, California 92704

World Airline Historical Society
13739 Picarsa Drive
Jacksonville, Florida 32225

 **Online Sites**

Aviation Digest
http://www.avdigest.com
Central site for aircraft
enthusiasts has hundreds
of links to other aircraft-
related sites.

Confederate Air Force
*http://www.avdigest.com/
caf/caf.html*
Home page of the world-
famous organization that
maintains World War II aircraft in flying condition.

National Air and
Space Museum
http://www.nasm.edu
Home page of the
Smithsonian museum for
aircraft.

Important Words

aileron movable part on an airplane's wing that lets the pilot roll the plane left or right

cockpit part of the airplane where the pilot sits and uses the controls

flap movable part on an airplane wing necessary to take off and land

fuselage main body of the airplane where the cabin and cockpit are located

radar instrument that uses electro-magnetic waves to detect airplanes in the air

rudder movable part attached to the tail that allows the pilot to steer the airplane

turboprop engine that uses jet propulsion to power the propeller

Index

Meet the Author

Darlene Stille resides in Chicago and is executive editor of the World Book Annuals. She has written several Children's Press books, including *Extraordinary Women Scientists*, *Extraordinary Women of Medicine*, and four other True Books on transportation.

Photo Credits ©: AP/Wide World Photos: 40; Arms Communications Inc.: 30 left (Ken Hammond), 9 left, 11 (Joseph Towers); Boeing Photo: 16, 24, 26 top, 27, 11 right inset (G. Thon); Corbis-Bettmann: 36 right; Gamma-Liaison: 43 right (Eric Brissaud), 2 (Tim Crosby), 20 left (Karl Gehring), cover, 23 bottom, 34 inset (Etienne de Malglaive), 23 top (Brian Smith); Office of Public Information, Lockheed-California Company: 41; Photo Researchers: 15 (David R. Frazier), 33 top (Jeff Greenberg), 8 (Joyce Photographics), 33 bottom (E. de Malglaive), 29 left (Porterfield/Chickering); Superstock, Inc.: 4, 9 right, 13, 17, 18 top, 20 right, 25, 26 bottom, 29 right, 34, 43 left; Tony Stone Images: 18 bottom (Paul Chesley), 30 right (Ross Harrison Koty), 11 left inset (Kevin Morris), 1 (Mark Wagner); UPI/Corbis-Bettmann: 36 left.